POETRY AND PROZAC

Also by the author in this series…

POETRY AND PROZAC

Poems about Depression

Leah Cass

Soul Revitalization LLC

Copyright © 2023 Leah Cass

ISBN: 978-1-960143-08-2

Contents

Dedication

This book is dedicated to the pain of my ancestors, and the anticipated joy of my progeny.

Preface

This is an ode to depression, or perhaps more accurately, a moment to acknowledge and embrace our pain. It is a journey that invites us to confront our inner struggles and accept their existence without judgment. It is an exploration of sadness and longing until we muster the courage to unravel its mysteries.

I have spent entirely too much of my life consumed by a longing to escape this world. Yet, standing here today, I can finally say I am happy to be alive. If this newfound appreciation is my sole achievement, then it was worth it.

Within these pages, we delve into the interconnectedness of human experience, the shared burden of suffering that unites us all. It is an exploration of our collective hurt and an affirmation that it is permissible to hold ourselves tenderly amid the complexities of existence.

Together, let us confront our pain, unlock its secrets, and discover the transformative power hidden within.

**Most Sinners have already been
through hell.**

MANIC

I get now

why people need medication

just to zombie shuffle through

the streets

I talked to the doctor

he said he can't make me happy

but he can dilute

the grief

Poetry and Prozac

The day

I went mad

It all left so swiftly

like only a tiny, frail

cord connected me

To sanity and truth

Tipping Point

Some things cause

more friction and

wear and tear

on the braided ropes

that hold us together

but don't ever forget

it could happen to you

We're All in This Together

I am stronger

than the demons

that plague my mind

that tell me lies

that make me blind

To the beauty that lies outside

I Hope

There is beauty in
the madness, too
In the piercing crystals
of her eyes

Sunset

No matter how hard I try

to bridge this chasm between us

I can't find a way

to the other side

and although I can barely see you

across the distance

but I can still feel your stare,

the love in your eyes

Just Around the Riverbend

I miss groceries the most
when I could drag you along
planning for cookouts
and parties and dinners on Tuesdays
you will carry on the bag as I
stocked our pantry shelves
pinterest dreams for dinner that nigh
A perfect illusion of a perfect little life
a perfect illusion of a perfect little wife

But you hate me now
and that store has closed
I found a new place to go

Bottom Dollar

I opened a book

While you opened

The bottle

Who knew

It would be

The death of us

Surprise

I've buried you in

the elusive corner

of my heart where I keep all of my secrets

I do not want to hear the clang of your

dry bones hitting the floor

when your skin has rotten away

Backbone

Sometimes I still remember

the way you smiled when you thought

I wasn't looking and how

I frowned the second

you began to walk away

Maybe in a distant dream

our eyes can meet

Face To Face

I have been searching

for the purge

that will forge

A bright new existence

where maybe I can be

born, clean again

But even in the absence of sin

underneath my smooth

baby skin

my heart is still wicked

Original Sin

Even my angels

Laugh and chant

Your name

When I beg

For a different

Direction

Jokes on Them

Sometimes we search

For those who break

Us open

We use

The flames to

Cauterize the bleeding

Wounds we've buried

Deep inside

Fireworks

It's a special kind of curse to be at once highly sensitive and to crave love but also to be unwilling or unable to compromise yourself or your values to fit in a box. For it is boxes people love.

I beg you

To suck the poison

Out of my skin

And tell me I

Can be clean

Again

Pretty Please with Sugar on Top

I know I'm diving into

Insanity again when I start

Writing poetry

Screen shotting poetry

Living, breathing

Poetry

The Dark Arts

There was beauty in her sadness because her heart told no lies.

MELANCHOLIA

Even my dreams
have become melancholy
and sorrow feels like home
after all this space and time

Space and Time

Our destiny has

Been hiding in the rafters

As we have started

Across the river

Searching for

Different answers

Alternatives

I've been searching for your

Absent smile

In this crowded sea

Of faces

Hoping to find

The idea of you

Again

Maybe I am crazy
I still believe in dreams

I still believe in you

When your brain
Starts telling you that
You are worthless

Alway Talk Back

Listen

For in times

Of fear

And heartbreak

Angels Speak

Where do our dreams go
when our hearts have been broken?
Where does our knowledge go
when our brains have crumbled into dust?
My faith has eroded
my hope has started to rust

Did Langston Know?

Maybe a riptide

can pull me into

the ocean and

I can drown

as the waves

crash over my body

finally home

I don't like it Here

I still see your face
in every empty space
I still hear your voice

In Silence

Maybe I can tweet and
write myself into sanity
into numbing the dull
lonely ache
I was meant to walk alone
This earth is not my home

Starseed

Maybe real life

no longer exists

we just post selfies

with the perfect lighting

and Google the perfect

witty responses and

hope to find a thing to fuck

before we scurry back

into our own corners

I Want Something Else to Get Me Through This

I still struggle with a
Universe that wont let me die
Or live no matter how
Many sacrifices I burn
On altars

I throw rocks at the
Sky in protest but
They fall back down and
Strike me instead

And god watches me bleed
In silence

But They Say I Gotta Have Faith

In the absence of
others do I even exist?
I've been wandering
on a cloud, alone
but now I've dissipated

Dissipated

If there is a god

Why can I not create

Beauty when my my

Brain is broken

The Ontological Question

I cried a million times

Over a destiny lost

And even my soul

Has had enough

Fin

I found you
Hidden in a
Corner of my heart
That I had forgotten
Existed

The tracks
Of my tears
Led me right
Back to you

Secrets

My brain has a bad habit
of visiting the places I put away
It taunts me with the possibilities
The it didn't have to be this ways
it won't let me free

My Brain

Sanity is often far too great a burden to bear.

PSYCHOTIC

My heart doesn't speak to me

It screams

Drowning out my mind's competition

Thorwing tantrums to get its desires

Burning bright red with fire

It will not be silenced

It will not be caged

Scream 3

I wonder sometimes

If my favorite

parts of me

are the ones that

make me sick

I don't want to

let them go

if that is so

I don't want to be better

Bipolar

How has time

Expanded

And

Contracted

All at once into this

Vicious loop of yesterday

Melting into

A million years

But a million years ago

Still feels like this moment

Since you've been gone

Grief

I didn't make it

This far in life

Only to be enslaved

By my own mind

My Heart is My Captor Instead

Sometimes in life

We are forced

To grieve

Someone who

Hasn't died

Or someone who didn't leave

If I Only Knew

How many words

I wish I could whisper

Into the quiet

But even sleep

Brings only

Deafening silence

Echos

Some lives

you sit on

the sidelines

in silence

and wait

for death

to overtake you

Is This Mine?

I think

I'm finally numb now

to this pain

to this desire

I've snuffed out

this flame

Extinguished

this fire

Linkin Park

Sometimes

I speak

to demons just

to hear your name

I've been searching

for forgiveness but

it didn't numb the pain

Guilt

Still time

has yet

to determine

if I'm

a sinner

or

a saint

Or Maybe I Don't Want to Know the Answer

God

I've forgotten

how to pray but

I will go on

my knees

if you take

these weak

demons away

Atheist Until I'm Drowning

I am nothing now

just bones and marrow

and mistakes

a breathing apparatus

inhaling and exhaling

the cosmos

take from me

my carbon dioxide is free

Rubbish Sale

I am

Formed of molten lava
cooling and hardening
under clear waters slowly
rising to the top
an island all alone
where only occasional castaways
wash up on shore

Wilson

My heart has been

Wide open for

Far too long

The gaping hole

Disconnected from my senses

So I sew it shut

Pricking my fingers with

The needle as I loop

Around the edges

Why Part 2

Once I held daisies

in my hands and

wore petunias

in my hair and

walked down

an aisle until

I ceased to exist

I Saw My Own Funeral

I want to lay

down in the street

and beg god

to take me

home where maybe I'll be free

My brain is broken

my heart is incomplete

I Don't Like It Here, Part 2

All my energy
has evaporated, floated
into the atmosphere
to be rained on
someone else
a different place
a different time

Sometimes I dream
of drowning
in the ocean
it hurt too much
to stay dry

Drowning

I made a pact with the devil
Just to feel your thoughts
And baby
You came up wanting

Cursed

I've been whispering

With the ghosts of my ancestors

They told me

I am the daughter of the

Whores who fought back

When you burned them

They taught me to smell

My grandfather's blood

On the coal in your furnace

Genealogy

Willfully

I climbed inside you

I'm not afraid of the dark

But you feared

My bravado

The light of my day

Bravado

There's a

You-shaped

Hole

In my heart

I've tried

To stuff it

Full but

Nothing else

Will fit

You

The greatest love

I've had

Was only imagined

It visits only

In dreams

So I Sleep

I cannot stop
Weaving these webs
When I've spent a
Thousand lives silent

How can I fear death?
I am the daughter
Of Osiris

Egypt

I wonder if
My brain and my
Heart miss
Each other in
The distance
I've forced
Between them

If they dream of
Getting coffee
Working together
Again
In the tandem of

Dancing to the
sway of
Relaxed music

Distance

POSTPARTUM AND ANTEPARTUM

I think maybe

I am still

The crying baby

Ripped from my

Mother's arms

And she kept

A piece of me

With her

A Motherless Daughter

And I think about my daughter

Wondering if after

All the stretch marks

And lost dinners if

She would have the audacity to look

Just like her father

With the don't leave me eyes

Spoiler: She Did

To speak a

Heart still whole

Repaired now, after

The dam

Break of its

Destruction

A life, now

Full

The sorrow of an empty womb

The pain of a surprisingly

Filled one

The rough touch of hands

These are a Few of My Favorite Things

The Buddhists say
You feel calm when you meet
Your soul mates and that's how I felt
When they first laid you on my chest

Peace for the first time
ever maybe
In this life

I'm sitting here
thinking about how
the love came
Later, exploding
out of my chest
The way that they talk
About in movies

I feel it when you
Stand on your tiptoes and
Offer me your hands
When I see your little face on
The grainy monitor, sleeping
Sweetly

I feel it when
I realize that you
Were always the plan

Aries, My North Node

I've been feeling my heart growing
Soft again

My knees weak again
Lips open again

You made me realize
Love
Is just your sleepy
Smile first thing in the morning

Tiny hands reaching for
My shirt without
Warning

Even the way you cry
When the tears are pouring

Sweet Child of Mine

I can feel my mother's heartbreak in my bones
I carry it
Because when I close my eyes
I am 3 years old and we are having a tea party
And she is letting me drink real tea
with lots of sugar

I carry my mother's heartbreak in my bones
Because I, too, am a mother and
if I cut the cords maybe my baby
Would too and i would deserve it
But couldn't take it

I carry my mother's heartbreak in my bones
Because i still don't know who I am
Without it

And my marrow aches to

Xylophones in the distance

Isis

Teach me how to

Serve in gried

Athena

teach me how to war

In peace

Lady Nada

teach my daughter

how to pray

I Don't Know What a Woman Is

Aphrodite

Help me shrink

And mend my womb

Stretched Thin

From letting broken men

Climb in

I don't know what

A woman is

Part 2

Maybe I'm destined, doomed

to pay for the sins of my mother

repeat her mistakes

She was charming and

funny and pretty

before she was consumed

by madness too

I Asked the Pastor

Let's entwine
our broken hearts
and feel alone together

Sure

I've been screaming

into a vacuum

until my voice

is lost and my

Ears go deaf but

I'll be dead

when you finally

hear me

Invisible

I have left pieces of me
in a single file line trailing
behind me

Eat your fill
they won't grow back
Completely

The Giving Tree

Sometimes only in rain

Can I feel alive

These pills make me fat but happy

Can I be loved

By you and me

At the same time?

Prozac

Hurry up

And make sure to get some rest

She says

Without offering to hold

The newborn

In my arms

Contractions and Contradictions

She is two years old

She tells me our home is lost
When we leave our driveway

And my bosom aches
Because she is home

And we are never lost
But this moment is

Time is a Thief

Ever time I hear a man

Mention he has children

I ask

Where are they now?

Who is watching them?

I tell him how lucky he is

That his children

Have such a good mother

Who is willing to help babysit

And that it's not easy being a man

Trying to have it all

Light peeks though

the window

birds cheerfully

taunting, their songs

so free

but I chose to be trapped in

this prison

paying penance eternal

for ample mistakes

Alcatraz

I asked him to

Tell me a secret

That I didn't know

He taught me that

Grief is just love

With nowhere to go.

And It Goes On and On and On

I thought maybe the broken

parts of you could overlap smoothly

into the broken parts of me

but we never crack that pretty

Our jagged edges collided

shattered, gritty

Shards of Broken Glass

And in that day

I was born

A mother

And you slept like a baby when you had forgotten my name.

CYCLOTHEMIA

I want to climb

to the top of

the highest mountains

and fill my lungs with

fresh, crisp air

and exhale into

screaming, purging, bleeding

until it all fades away

I don't trust myself heights

but maybe if I touch the sky

I'll be closer to your light

and maybe god will hear me there

Isaac on the Mountain

If energy can be neither created
Nor destroyed
Where did yours go?
Do you hear me
When I cry out your name
Or do my tears just water the earth
To which your flesh has returned
Nourishing the flowers
While your box sits
Dark and empty

Or is this you
This presence I always feel
Inside and near me

I have to know

Dad

I've lost

All the contents of

My pockets

I'd collected before

I went to the market

To sell my soul

But the devil

Doesn't want it

Anymore

No Take Backs

And the miles between us

Could be crossed with a single

Step but neither of us will ever

Give in

Babies

I've become a soul
Without a country
This world
Is not my home

Lonely

From that wellspring of hope

Came only destruction

I burned in the flames

Of its flickering light

Now nourish your garden

With my water and ashes

Maybe in death

I can get something right

Fertilizer

I think I'm destined

Doomed

To walk alone

Under the cover

Of nightfall

Arms outstretched

And always empty

Empty

Some days
I miss you more
Like the moon
Pulling the tides
Of my love
Back and forth

Lunatic

I don't fit well

In cages my spirit

Leaks through the bars

Polluting the air

With my scent

Prison

When I die

Plant me with a

Tree so I can

Grow in all the ways

I never could

In peace

Growth Never Ends

All the stars
And galaxies and
Molecules and
People twirl
And buzz
And hum and
Intertwine

But in this earth
I stand alone
Not one of them
Is mine

I Stand Alone

I laid with you

In darkness

Held your hand

And kissed your head

But when dawn broke

You, my reflection

Were a stranger in my bed

Twins

I always tried

To do the right thing

Even all alone

But now I know I

Should have chosen

You

At the Fork in the Road

I still see your face
In every empty space
I still hear your voice

In Silence

Sometimes

I still ache

In the parts of me

You burned away

They've stopped being real

Just Phantom Pain

Maybe it's only

My danger

That keeps me safe

My crazy

That keeps me

Sane

Learned Behavior

I know now

Why people

Lock their hearts

In cages and

Throw away

The key

Knowledge is Power

Never forget

Depression is

Only a stop

A part of your journey

Never the Destination

Acknowledgments

I would not be anywhere without my family. Thank you to Bill, Kaylee, Eliza, Vanessa, William, Jason, and Lois. Huge thank you to Aimee, who helped me edit and format and calmed me down when I needed it. Special shout out to Instagram as well, and all the followers who believed in me when I was just sad and trying to feel better. Thank you to my soul family, for believing in me and always encouraging me. And thank you to my dad. I wish you were still here to see it

End Notes

1. This series is an homage to the five stages of grief model was developed by **Elisabeth Kübler-Ross**, and became famous after she published her book On Death and Dying in 1969.

2. Chapters are based on different types of depression.

3. Page 43- Reference to "A Dream Deferred" by Langston Hughes.

4. Page 93- Reference to "Bible on the Dash" by Gunplay.

5. Page 116 – "Lunacy- a kind of insanity supposedly dependent on the phases of the moon."

About The Author

Leah Cass is a poet, writer, mental health advocate, and lover of all things spiritual. She currently resides in Pittsburgh, PA with her husband, daughter, and two spoiled cats. She graduated from Chatham University with a bachelor's degree in Psychology and continued her education in clinical mental health counseling at Duquesne University.

A strong believer in the power of story to build community and spark healing, Leah loves using her voice to help others open up about their own experiences with mental health and personal growth. She frequently speaks at events and workshops on topics such as mental health awareness, post traumatic growth, and self-care. You can find her on Instagram as @elleunchained.

Also About The Author

Made in the USA
Monee, IL
13 May 2024

58395741R00069